theme

character

technique

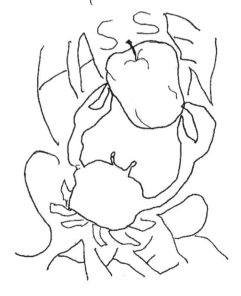

CONSOLATION SNACKS

HASSEN SAKER

furniture press books

FURNITURE PRESS BOOKS

Edited by Christophe Casamassima

First Furniture Press Edition 2017

Copyright © 2017 hassen saker

All Rights Reserved

Furniture Press Books titles are distributed

to the trade by Small Press Distribution

spdbooks.org

Cover and Interior Images: Don Riggs

Layout by Christophe Casamassima

Manufactured in the United States of America

ISBN: 978-1-940092-17-1

furniture.press.books@gmail.com

CONSOLATION SNACKS

*Warmest thanks to
Jared Hassen, Ethel Rackin, and Lauren Cavote.*

contraindication

pre face

this is what i know about myself

dispassion

.

cool is not hot

narcissist's joke

i'm only kidding myself

fence made from the tree of knowledge

intrinsic barrier

under
mine

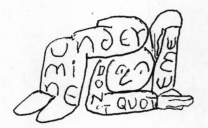

pointless problem

i keep going nonlinear

hell's angels

isn't anarchy inherently ironic

contraindication

addiction to addiction

fractal stutter

hesitation when every word's
a potential labyrinth

lightning

frenetic static

deadpan

expression by omission

hidden
nature

poetic cliché

if the latter, not the former

inconceivable poetry

pregnant silence

lingerie poems

"inaccessible" "obscure"

quote jokes

"poetry business"

under mine

"don't quote me"

acquired taste

dangerously adapting palate during
scarcity becomes "delicacy"

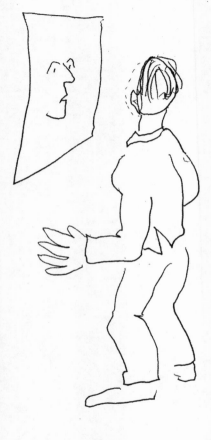

pre-face

market label: "disposable"

flagged for obsolescent convenience
or convenient obsolescence

the [anti]christian right

proselytize misanthropy

corporate efficiency

making humanity obsolete

privatized heart emoticon

$

perpetuation of perpetration

accuse the accuser

mathematics of a mediocracy

dominated by the lowest common
denominator

criminal spin

bound for no boundaries

human acclimation

climate change accelerator

psychosis

gross shadow schematic

psychological avoidance consequence

the self-fulfilled prophecy

emotional crutches

bridging voids

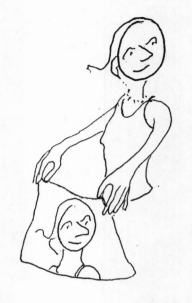

Existential
decoy

tar baby

the term itself as a self-inflicted disaster

existential decoy

identity

stein & scripture

there's no there-there

borges loo reading

appropriate convolutions

exploiting survival

noncoital orgasm

Exploiting Survival

groundwork for orientation

define "up"

shot in the dark

describe the smell

any matter

every color but the ones you see

chromatophore hue

default = true

nothing is completely ambiguous

truth

hidden nature

gene suppression

chagrin of arrogance

never looking up the pronunciation

BORGES LOO READING

nouveau riche

do they even know what this means

punk

shaking up your shit

real punk

bomb "due diligence"

punk participation

NECESSARY REACTIVITY

comfort in nonconformity

lucky punk

not talking nonsense to empty chairs
on stage in front of large audiences

penultimate postmodernism

loathing my self-consciousness

ultimate postmodernism

disgust with the loathing of
my self-consciousness

if a tree falls in the forest

what did the coprolaliac say to
the paranoid schizophrenic?

ironically thick as thieves

many narcissists seem to
really love each other

Shot
in the
dark

cannon-canon

phallus-fallacy

proprioception

evolutionary palimpsest

absurdism contingency

hope springs eternal

consolation prize

my comic strip expression of horror

la petite mort

rubbed out

wake

damage control

pigeonhole

boobytrap

dirty trick

paralysis by ambition

ostensible humility

VARIOUS SNARES

pretentiously unpretentious

a bumbling portage

deciding how to decide

chinese finger trap

playing the victim

crying wolf

critical fatigue

mirage

clarity in delirium

Dispassion

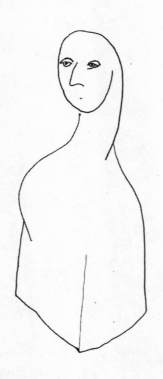

dogma

leave the thinking to us

born again

shirking adult responsibility

existential footing

GLOSSOLALIA

not my fault

sentience

a messy mutation

successful counterculture

culture

taste bud

evolved over kill

golden age prerequisite

golden rule

unbearable nausea

haunting by your idiot self

unbearable hilarity

sic your personal mime

artifice arithmetic

it's the thought that counts

freudian underslip

is my ego showing?

Stein and Scripture

the singularity

rapture or babylon

artificial intelligence

superficial biomimicry

artificial insinuation

program semiotics of nothingness

artificial challenge

how to code entelechy

artificial inspiration

think outside the box, box

camouflaged latin in-autological question

where's cognito

conceptually autological question

what's the mystery club about

aging autological question

QUESTIONING THE QUESTION

what's that memory game called

complete question

what is the inquiry process

trick question

are you honest with yourself

nothing is complete
nothing is complete

fraud

mime this

dumb[founded]

fake your speech test

.

a word is to a ratio as

tomboy kid

a dress is something you put on a wound

pubescent tomboy

a bra is something that separates you

adolescent tomboy

a period is the unstoppable stop

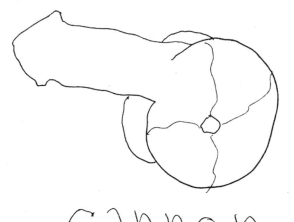

cannon

canon

primal screams

ageless self-birthing

can of worms

don't start or don't stop

mirror

real fake

strange attractor

the forecast changes like the weather

fuzzy linguistics

RIDES AT THE PHYSICS AMUSEMENT PARK

hypothoses

joker's wild

quanta like a simile

now what

here we are all bumped up against the big bang

[anti]revelation

a slight turn of events on little bang day

tevatron piñata

RIDES AT THE PHYSICS AMUSEMENT PARK

candy matter!

quantum attitude

half empty or half full

field theories

RIDES AT THE PHYSICS AMUSEMENT PARK

varying degrees of in[n/t]er states

fulcrum liberation

frees as opposed to freeze

QUOTE
JOKES

credentials

character metrics

pollyanna principle

negate negativity

superstition

inductive validity

possibly positive double negative

anti-depressant

loyalty to proletariat

reluctant pandering

algorithm rodeo

pattern wrangling

meta fog

<THIS MEANS META>

a deer blind, or a deer in headlights

meta siblings

<THIS MEANS META>

(parenthetic) #hashtag

meta fail

zen instruction

meta realism

<THIS MEANS META>

the usefulness of hope

meta theater

<THIS MEANS META>

chorus run amok

dissociation

inverted quarantine

vanishing point

infinite allusion

antibacterial

biohazard boomerang

Freudian
Underslip

false guilt

temptation of alternate realities

seek truth

read between the li[n]es

deconstructivist art

VOID

b^n

power-power

love

bio logic

generosity 101

acknowledging another's reality

humanity for dummies

CORE CURRICULUM

guerrilla lovefare

prerequisite for potential

reconciliation w/demons

random acts of kindness

abracadabra

appropriately addressed contrition

human acclmation

perfection

red herring

editorial adventures in neuroplasticity

i've changed my mind

smirk

because language facilitates vomiting